I KNOW WHAT TO DO! SOCIAL SKILLS

HOW TO WORK TOGETHER

CAITIE MCANENEY

PowerKiDS press

Published in 2025 by The Rosen Publishing Group, Inc.
2544 Clinton Street, Buffalo, NY 14224

First Edition

Editor: Caitie McAneney
Book Design: Rachel Rising

Photo Credits: Cover, pp. 1, 11 Evgeny Atamanenko/Shutterstock.com; pp. 4, 6, 8, 10, 11, 12, 14, 16, 18, 20 Cute art/Shutterstock.com; p. 5 New Africa/Shutterstock.com; p. 7 Gorodenkoff/Shutterstock.com; p. 9 Ground Picture/Shutterstock.com; p. 13 ESB Professional/Shutterstock.com; p. 15 Trzykropy/Shutterstock.com; p. 17 suchalinee/Shutterstock.com; p. 19 Olena Yakobchuk/Shutterstock.com; p. 21 PeopleImages.com - Yuri A/Shutterstock.com.

Library of Congress Cataloging-in-Publication Data
McAneney, Caitie, author. Title: How to work together / Caitie McAneney. Description: Buffalo, NY : PowerKids Press, 2025. | Series: I know what to do! social skills | Includes index. Identifiers: LCCN 2024034170 (print) | LCCN 2024034171 (ebook) | ISBN 9781499450637 (library binding) | ISBN 9781499450620 (paperback) | ISBN 9781499450644 (ebook) Subjects: LCSH: Group work in education–Juvenile literature. | Helping behavior in children–Juvenile literature. | Teamwork (Sports)–Juvenile literature. | Social learning–Juvenile literature. | Social skills–Juvenile literature. Classification: LCC LB1032 .M422 2025 (print) | LCC LB1032 (ebook) | DDC 371.3/602855376–dc23/eng/20240725 LC record available at https://lccn.loc.gov/2024034170 LC ebook record available at https://lccn.loc.gov/2024034171

Manufactured in the United States of America

CPSIA Compliance Information: Batch #CWPK25. For Further Information contact Rosen Publishing at 1-800-237-9932.

CONTENTS

Working Together

Have you ever seen ants working together? Each tiny ant does its part. They collect and store food for their community. People need to work together too! Sports teams work together. Companies work together. Bands work together. You can do a lot as a team!

Many Hands

There's an old saying. "Many hands make light work." Think about cleaning up a classroom. There are toys and craft supplies everywhere! It's a lot for one person to clean. If you all work together, it can be done quickly and easily.

Brainstorm!

You may have a big problem to solve. You may have a creative **project** to do. You can work together to think up ideas. That's called brainstorming. Set your goals. Then share your ideas. Together, you can figure it out.

Listening and Sharing

What skills do you need to work as a team? You need to listen and share. Listen to another person's ideas. **Consider** their idea. Give helpful **feedback**. Then, share your own idea or build on their idea. Always be kind and helpful with your words.

PRACTICE MAKES PROGRESS!

To share ideas, you can say:

"Do you have an idea for solving the problem?"

"I never thought of it that way!"

"I like your idea. Maybe we could also ..."

"I have an idea. What if we ...?"

Special Strengths

Everyone has special skills and strengths. Imagine you're packing a picnic. Maybe one friend is good at making sandwiches. Another friend chooses fruit. Another friend **organizes** the basket. Use everyone's special strengths!

Helping at Home

Families have to work together at home. They can work together to keep their space clean. Maybe one person sweeps. Another person washes dishes. Another person does **laundry**. You can even work together to make dinner!

Teamwork at School

You may be part of a school project. Maybe it's a learning project. Maybe it's an art project. You might be in a big group or in a pair. You plan the project together. Everyone can share **resources** and do some of the work.

Dealing with Differences

Sometimes working together is hard. You might have different ideas. You might do things different ways. This can lead to **conflict**. Talk it out. See how you can each give up a little of what you want until you agree. That's called compromise.

Go Team!

The ability to work together is important. You can learn more and do more together. You can also have more fun! You may need an adult's help to figure things out. That's okay. Ask for help when you need it. Remember you're on the same team!

GLOSSARY

conflict: A struggle or disagreement between people.

consider: To think about something seriously.

feedback: Helpful information that someone gives to show what can be improved.

laundry: Clothing, sheets, and other things that you wash.

organize: To set in order.

project: An activity that takes effort and planning.

resource: Something that can be used.

FOR MORE INFORMATION

BOOKS

Colich, Abby. *Encouraging Others*. Minneapolis, MN: Blue Owl Books, 2022.

Rose, Rachel. *Let's Pull Together*. Solon, OH: Playaway Products, LLC, 2024.

WEBSITES

Animal Teamwork
www.timeforkids.com/k1/animal-teamwork/
Learn more about how animals use teamwork in the wild.

Simple Teamwork Games
www.pbs.org/parents/crafts-and-experiments/simple-teamwork-games
Explore these games and activities with your parents or teachers to practice teamwork!

INDEX